Rookie Read-About® Civics

We Are Better Together

Ann Bonwill

Content Consultant

Elizabeth Case DeSantis, M.A. Elementary Education

Julia A. Stark Elementary School, Stamford, Connecticut

Reading Consultant

Jeanne M. Clidas, Ph.D.

Reading Specialist

Children's Press®

An Imprint of Scholastic Inc.

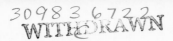

3098 36722

Library of Congress Cataloging-in-Publication Data
Names: Bonwill, Ann, author.
Title: We are better together/By Ann Bonwill.
Description: New York: Children's Press, An Imprint of Scholastic Inc., 2019. |
Series: Rookie read-about civics | Includes index.
Identifiers: LCCN 2018032591| ISBN 9780531129128 (library binding) | ISBN 9780531137703 (pbk.)
Subjects: LCSH: Interpersonal relations—Juvenile literature. | Interpersonal relations in children—Juvenile literature.
Classification: LCC HM1106 .B66 2019 | DDC 302—dc23

Produced by Spooky Cheetah Press
Design: Keith Plechaty/kwpCreative
Creative Direction: Judith E. Christ for Scholastic Inc.

Published in 2019 by Children's Press, an imprint of Scholastic Inc.

Printed in North Mankato, MN, USA   113

1 2 3 4 5 6 7 8 9 10 R 28 27 26 25 24 23 22 21 20 19

Scholastic, Inc., 557 Broadway, New York, NY 10012.

Photographs © cover: momentimages/Getty Images; cover flag bunting: LiveStock/Shutterstock; 3: Rawpixel.com/Shutterstock; 4 top left: Jayme Thornton/Getty Images; 4 bottom left: 120b_rock/iStockphoto; 4 remaining: Rawpixel.com/Shutterstock; 7: monkeybusinessimages/iStockphoto; 9 background: irin-k/Shutterstock; 9 girl in kimono: ULTRA.F/Getty Images; 9 boy in white: uniquely india/Getty Images; 9 girl in hijab: Joko Prayitno/EyeEm/Getty Images; 9 boy in jeans: Wavebreakmedia/iStockphoto; 9 girl in sari: uniquely india/Getty Images; 10: lisegagne/iStockphoto; 13: Huntstock/age fotostock; 15: Fertnig/iStockphoto; 16: wavebreakmedia/Shutterstock; 19: sturti/iStockphoto; 21: kali9/iStockphoto; 22: Richard Hutchings/PhotoEdit; 25: Paul Bradbury/Caiaimage/Getty Images; 27: FatCamera/iStockphoto; 28: AP Images; 29 flag: nazlisart/Shutterstock; 30 clipboard: pikepicture/Shutterstock; 30 eraser: domnitsky/Shutterstock; 30 pencil: Vectorpocket/Shutterstock; 31 top right: FatCamera/iStockphoto; 31 center right soapbox racer: sturti/iStockphoto; 31 center right selfie: lisegagne/iStockphoto; 31 bottom right background: irin-k/Shutterstock; 31 bottom right girl in kimono: ULTRA.F/Getty Images; 31 bottom right boy in white: uniquely india/Getty Images; 31 bottom right girl in hijab: Joko Prayitno/EyeEm/Getty Images; 31 bottom right boy in jeans: Wavebreakmedia/iStockphoto; 31 bottom right girl in sari: uniquely india/Getty Images.

Table of Contents

CHAPTER 1

Look at Us

Red, black, brown, blond. Even bald! Do you see our hair? It is curly, kinky, and straight. It is in braids, ponytails, and buzz cuts. We all have hair, but it is not all the same.

How do you wear your hair?

Our eyes are blue, brown, and green. Our skin is dark, light, and in between. We are all different. We are all beautiful.

 Do you have the same color eyes as any of your friends?

What cool clothes! We wear saris, jeans, and hijabs. On special occasions we put on kimonos, kilts, and jingle dresses. We all wear clothes, but we are all **unique**. There is no one just like you!

 What do you wear on holidays?

CHAPTER 2

Look at Our Families

Who is in our family? We come from **diverse** families, big and small. We might have five siblings or none at all. We might live with a grandma, a stepdad, or two moms.

Who is in your family?

Hola! Salaam! Hello! We all communicate, but not always in the same way. Our families speak different languages. Some families use their hands to speak sign language.

Just like our languages, our foods are different, too. Tacos or curry? Pasta or pita? It all sounds yummy!

 What language does your family speak at home?

This means "let's play" in American Sign Language.

We live in apartments, townhomes, and houses. We have big yards, small yards, and yards on the roof! We all need shelter, but the places where we live might not look alike. A farm, a skyscraper, and a cabin in the woods can all be called home.

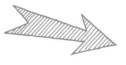 Do you live in the city, the country, or the suburbs?

CHAPTER 3

Look What We Can Do

We all like to learn. But we don't all learn in the same ways. Some kids like math. Others like reading. Some kids use computers to communicate. Some have a helper in the classroom.

 What is your favorite subject in school?

There are so many fun ways to play. We run, jump, and roll. We play pretend and freeze tag and chess. We all love to have fun!

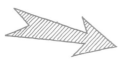 What games do you like to play alone or with your friends?

Even though we are different, we all have love in our hearts. We love our families, our friends, and our pets. And they love us back, with a hug, a high five, or a big lick!

How do you show people you love them?

CHAPTER 4

Better Together

What would happen if we were all the same? We would not be able to learn from each other and try new things. We would not be challenged to think about the world in different ways.

 What have you learned from people who are different from you?

We can be friends with people who are a lot like us. And we can be friends with people who are different from us, too. With a different friend, we might eat egg rolls for the first time. We might try a new activity, like ice-skating, for the first time. We might sleep over in sleeping bags, bunk beds, or a tent in the backyard.

 **What do you like to do with your friends?**

Good friends care about each other. We listen, share, and play peacefully. We might fight sometimes, but we **compromise** and **cooperate** to work things out.

No matter how different or alike we are, one thing is for sure: We are better together!

 How does having lots of friends who are all different make your life better?

I Have

Martin Luther King Jr. was a leader.
He taught people to respect differences.
In 1963, Dr. King gave a speech in
Washington, D.C. He talked about a
dream he had for the future. He hoped
that someday
people with
different skin colors
could live, learn,
work, and play
together peacefully.
His words remind
us that we are
better together.

a Dream

Here's part of Dr. King's "I Have a Dream" speech:

66 I have a dream that my four little children will one day live in a nation where they will not be judged by the color of their skin but by the content of their character . . .

66 I have a dream that . . . little black boys and black girls will be able to join hands with little white boys and white girls as sisters and brothers.

66 I HAVE A DREAM TODAY . . . 99

© 1963 Martin Luther King, Jr.; www.archives.gov/files/press/exhibits/dream-speech.pdf

How to Make a New Friend

It isn't hard to do! Just follow these simple steps...

- ☑ Always start by saying "hello."

- ☑ Ask someone new to play with you at recess or after school.

- ☑ Share your toys with your friends.

- ☑ Be considerate of other people's feelings.

- ☑ Listen to what others have to say.

- ☑ Include everyone in the fun—no one likes to be left out!

Glossary

compromise (**kahm**-pruh-mize): **to accept just some of what you want to satisfy some requests of others**
▶ *Friends* **compromise** *when deciding what to play.*

cooperate (koh-**ah**-peh-rate): **to work together toward the same goal**
▶ *Good friends know how to* **cooperate***.*

diverse (di-**vers**): **having many different types or kinds; varied**
▶ *Having a* **diverse** *group of friends makes life more fun.*

unique (yoo-**neek**): **the only one of its kind; unlike anything else**
▶ *You and your friends have a lot in common, but each of you is* **unique***!*

31

Index

Facts for Now

Visit this Scholastic website for more information on diversity:

www.factsfornow.scholastic.com

Enter the keywords **Better Together**

About the Author

Ann Bonwill enjoys writing books for children. She lives in a house in the suburbs with her husband, son, and corgi dog.